A Day with Police Officers

By Jan Kottke

Welcome
Books

Children's Press
A Division of Grolier Publishi
New York / London / Hong Kong /
Danbury, Connecticut

D1384538

Photo Credits: Cover, p. 5, 7, 9, 13, 17, 21 by Thaddeus Harden; p. 11 © FPG; p. 15, 19 © Corbis
Contributing Editor: Jennifer Ceaser
Book Design: Michael DeLisio

Visit Children's Press on the Internet at:
http://publishing.grolier.com

Library of Congress Cataloging-in-Publication Data

Kottke, Jan.
  A day with police officers / by Jan Kottke.
      p.   cm.—(Hard work)
  Includes bibliographical references and index.
  Summary: Illustrations and simple text describe different kinds of police officers and
the work they do.
  ISBN 0-516-23092-1 (lib. bdg.)— ISBN 0-516-23017-4 (pbk.)
  1. Police—Juvenile literature. [1. Police.] I. Title.
HV7922 .K67 2000
363.2'023'73—dc21

                                                                        00-020654

Contents

We are **police officers**.

We help people.

We keep people safe.

4

5

We start our day at the **police station**.

We find out where we will **patrol** that day.

I patrol the roads.

I make sure people don't break the **law**.

I have to write a **ticket** if a person drives too fast.

We patrol on horses.

There's a big **parade** today.

We make sure that people march safely.

I patrol on a boat.

I make sure that everyone is being safe in the water.

I patrol on a bike.

I ride my bike through the park.

I make sure everyone in the park is safe.

14

I work in the street.

I use my hands to tell cars when to stop and go.

I make sure people cross the street safely.

17

I patrol with Buster.

Buster is a police dog.

Buster helps me look for **clues**.

19

Sometimes I stop and talk to people.

They thank me for keeping them safe.

I'm happy to help them.

New Words

clues (klooz) things that help police figure out when someone has done something wrong

law (law) a rule that people must follow

parade (puh-**rayd**) a group of people that march together down a street

patrol (puh-**trol**) to keep a place safe

police officers (puh-**leese aw**-fih-sirz) people who make sure others are safe and follow laws

police station (puh-**leese stay**-shen) a place where police officers work

ticket (**tik**-it) something given to a driver who breaks the law

To Find Out More

Books
Officer Brown Keeps Neighborhoods Safe
by Alice K. Flanagan
Children's Press

Officer Buckle and Gloria
by Peggy Rathmann
Putnam Publishing

Police Officers (In My Neighborhood)
by Paulette Bourgeois, Kim Lafave, and Peter Bourgeois
General Distribution Services

Web Site
Super Trooper
http://www.users.fast.net/~louis2/index.html
This site has information about police officers and the equipment they use.
It also includes important safety tips.

Index

About the Author

Jan Kottke is the owner/director of several preschools in the Tidewater area of Virginia. A lifelong early education professional, she is completing a phonics reading series for preschoolers.

Reading Consultants

Kris Flynn, Coordinator, Small School District Literacy, The San Diego County Office of Education

Shelly Forys, Certified Reading Recovery Specialist, W.J. Zahnow Elementary School, Waterloo, IL

Peggy McNamara, Professor, Bank Street College of Education, Reading and Literacy Program